My Mother's Poem and Other Songs

My Mother's Poem and Other Songs

Songs and Poems

Micere Githae Mugo

EAST AFRICAN EDUCATIONAL PUBLISHERS
NAIROBI

Published by
East African Educational Publishers
Brick Court
Westlands
Mpaka Road/Woodvale Grove
P. O. Box 45314
Nairobi

First Published 1994
© Micere Githae Mugo 1994

ISBN 9966-46-499-9

Printed by
General Printers Ltd,
Homa Bay Road,
P.O. Box 18001, Nairobi, Kenya.
G0258

For my mother,
Grace Njeri
who embodies
all the attributes
of Mother Africa's
Matriots

Contents

Acknowledgements

I am grateful to the Rockefeller Foundation for giving me the generous award that allowed me to take sabbatical leave and leave of absence from my heavy duties at the University of Zimbabwe, in order to work on this and other manuscripts that had been sitting under the heavy volume of my professional work for years. Special thanks go to Dr David Court, the Director of the Africa Regional Office in Nairobi who, with charactersitic concern and empathy, listened to the story that led to my applying for the grant. His efficiency, friendly support and dependability are a source of back-up energy when one is working on a project such as this one.

The Africana Studies and Research Center, Cornell University, provided the academic home and environment that allowed me to do the necessary research work on some of the pieces, as well as the fora at which I read a number of the creations to appreciative audiences. A long time mindset of fear and terror, on my part, before the mysteries of a computer, eventually found resolution during my time at Africana. I now feel liberated on this front and more than grateful to Africana for allowing me the old computer that did the trick.

My daughters, Mumbi and Njeri combined, make an invaluable network of support with their unfailing solidarity, loyalty, support and understanding, often having to fend for themselves and for me, as I keep long, long hours in the office, even during the weekends. They have provided sanity for me many times during our difficult period in exile.

To my sister, colleague and friend, Amandina Lihamba, who agreed not only to read through the manuscript, but to write an introduction at a time when her time during her sabbatical leave was fully mortgaged, I say *shukrani*!

The entire responsibility for the preparation and cooking of the creative menus in this volume is mine and mine alone and I take complete responsibility for whatever may be raw, unpalatable, or undigestible in any of the dishes before you.

Africana Studies and Research Center
Cornell University, New York.
March 1993

Preface

My first collection of poetry, 'Daughter of My People Sing!' appeared in 1966, through the East African Literature Bureau, which with the sad breaking up of the East African Community, became the Kenya Literature Bureau. Since then there has been one persistent question from my readers: When is the next collection coming out? The present volume of poems is my belated response to that positively nagging question.

Between mothering my daughters, bringing them up, being a single head of household, negotiating around nomadic existence in exile, engaging in political activism and answering the call of academia, especially its gospel of 'publish or perish' (really meaning: publish research scholarship or be doomed), I have found myself simply having to shelve the creative writing project over the years. *My Mother's Poem and Other Songs* thus comes after a gap of five years since I published a children's play, *Zamani and Sifiso*, as a part of the Zimbabwe Schools Readers Series, with the Curriculum Development Unit, Ministry of Education. Luckily, an award by the Rockefeller Foundation has provided me with the financial means and space to rescue rough drafts of creative writing, including the poems in this volume, that were gathering dust on my shelves, awaiting polishing up for publication.

While finalizing and re-writing the songs and poems in this collection, I have become abundantly conscious of the indebtedness I owe to my brother, friend and colleague, Okelo Oculi, the Ugandan poet and political scientist, who first introduced me to the concept of 'exploding silences' as a major task in poetry composition. I have used this concept extensively over the last twenty years, only adding to it the notion of positive versus negative silences. The reason for this modification is that, in my judgement, there is an important case to be made for positive silences. They are willed and not imposed. They are, in fact, desirable. They constitute the delineation of necessary space which we consciously create around our lives from time to time, as a means of regrouping and replenishing our emotional needs, revitalizing our imaginative and intellectual energies, recharging the battery of life when the level goes low. Thus we may deliberately choose to be silent, as we reflect, organize our thoughts and feelings, take stock of a given situation and so on. In other words, we take a planned retreat, sketch commas, dictate full-stops, curve question marks and emphasize the exclamation marks of our lives. Positive and voluntary silences are enriching and rejuvenating, not suffocating. On the other hand negative silences are enforced upon us by stifling conditions in life, characterized by domination, negation, prescription, dictation, discrimination, oppression, exploitation, exclusion, marginalization and other forms of human rights abuse at the econo-political, social-cultural, gender, class and other levels. Negative silences deny their victims the most basic of basic human rights: *being*, meaning, the unconditional right to self-determine their lives through unhindered participation in the production process and in this way realize their full human potential.

If Okelo Oculi had claimed copy rights around the concept of 'exploding silences' when he came up with it in the sixties, I would have been faced with a steep fee to pay for my borrowing. Twenty years is a long time, even in terms of a soft loan! In fact, three years ago, this burden of borrowing became so heavy that I wrote to Okelo, asking him in the name of comradeship, never to think of suing me! Happily too, since acquainting myself with his coinage and specifically during the last two years, I have come across explorations of the same motif by others. The most notable of these has been that of the late Audrey Lorde, whose essay, 'The Transformation of Silence into Language and Action' in her book, *The Cancer Journals*, is a shining piece.

Ayi Kwei Armah's *The Beautyful Ones Are Not Yet Born* has provided another text that I have had continuing dialogue with, agreeing that the neo-colonial ruling class truly does constitute a bunch of ugly creatures of prey, but insisting that even in the midst of all this ugliness, beautiful human beings have been born and continue to be born. Indeed beautiful births have been taking place in this contradictory world of ours since time immemorial and more are still on the way or under conception. What is needed is the evolution of systems that will enhance this beauty, instead of destroying it, systems that will rid us of the ugly lot and their ugliness, systems that will create human beings to replace the ogres running it, systems that will evolve and celebrate true human values inspite of the limitations inherent in us as mortal beings. I have faith that it is within the human capacity to do this. To overcome the beast in us, while promoting the 'angel' beyond the tissue-thin line that divides the two, and here I am borrowing from Platt, the Canadian poet.

The other influence that continues to engage my creativity is the importance of the role of orature and popular art within the African context. This engagement has been re-inforced by my involvement in community and people's theatre, especially during my stay in Zimbabwe where I have been a cultural worker with Zambuko/Izibuko for the last few years. Our dramatized texts have at times included poetry which has gone down extremely well with the audiences we have performed to. The appreciation of dramatized poetry, by often predominantly mass audiences, has left me persuaded that the aversion to poetry which is viewed as an impossible genre of literature in schools, colleges and universities, comes from the deliberate enigmatism imposed upon the readers through texts essentially designed to sit on academic shelves.

At the risk of overstating my case, I wish to pay tribute to those ethics and aesthetics of African Orature, as a popular art form, that are positive and progressive. I have borrowed heavily from these in composing the poems collected here. Two of my recent publications: *African Orature and Human Rights*, as well as the introduction to Emmanuel Ngara's fine volume of poetry, *Songs from the Temple*, explain the importance I place upon this progressive 'return to the source' in the spirit of Amilcar Cabral's advocacy. The need to address this concern, coupled with my intimated involvement in community theatre, has led me to consciously work towards liberating my poetry from abstraction and enigmatism, insisting that communication and participation assume a central role in the dialogical process. The compositions in this collection deliberately go out of their way to try and embrace the audience as part of the creative process. More than that many of them reach out from the shelves, insisting on dramatization and performance.

As is evident, I continue to be on the side of functional art in the ongoing debate on the role of art and the artist in society. However, I also firmly believe that this emphasis should not be an excuse for sloppiness in form. Serious functional art should strive for as much stylistic innovation and originality as possible if the content it seeks to convey is to claim the definition of genuine art.

And now onto a practical illustration that makes the final point on this issue of popular art. Following readings of some of the poems in this collection to American audiences, some of my listeners, have commented on the fact that the poetry is too focused on the oppression of the masses and their struggles. A few have even asked me whether I ever write poetry on love and other 'non-political' themes. My response has been that within the context of exploitation and powerlessness experienced by the impoverished majority in Africa, the so-called Third World and the rest of this planet called earth, love is a very political theme. I say, for the poor there is no private space to even engage in love making! True, my poetry is heavy; but so is marginal existence for the majority of my people.

This said, I also hope that the optimism that I always seek to infuse my poetic statements with comes through, for, there is no doubt in my mind that with networking and the linking of global struggles, the dispossessed of this world will ultimately succeed in asserting their humanity, even though the achievement of this may be a lifelong process.

Micere Githae Mugo
Africana Studies and Research Center
Cornell University, New York, U.S.A.
March, 1993.

Introduction

The history of contemporary African art, literature and criticism has been one which has tried to come to terms with the post-colonial reality. This is a reality which has been characterized by cultural crisis — a crisis nurtured and sharpened by repression, oppression and exploitation, endemic in post-colonial economic and political systems at regional and global levels. In its multitude of manifestations, the crisis has provided thematic content for creative impulses in various forms. Of greater interest, however, have been the perspectives and functions the creations have taken as exhibited through their forms, content and context of production. In these, neither the creators nor the critics have always been in agreement. The contentions and the inconsistencies of positions displayed in creative and critical works have not only been the result of the creative dynamism of Africa's creative output but also of the contending ideologies and literary paradigms which have tried to define and situate aesthetics, creative processes, cultural practice and the forms it takes within Africa's contemporary reality as well as the different visions for the continent's direction towards cultural disalienation and liberation.

Reading the poems contained in this volume, one is brought again face to face with some of the critical issues and notions in contemporary African literary discourse. Unlike many creative works that display ambivalence, ambiguity and obfuscation in content and perspective, the poems, as a collective, carry a clarity of their creative context, political and aesthetic intentions. Continually, the cultural crisis and the struggles it engenders insist themselves as reference, framework, focal points and thematic concern. For in an Amilcar Cabral sense, the author makes it clear that Africa continues to be in a liberation struggle until it can effect 'the liberation of productive forces and consequently the ability to determine the mode of production most appropriate to the evolution of liberated peoples'. The poems, therefore, display an unapologetic and unwavering stance of the author's position and the perspectives she gives to the notions of the role of literature and art in this liberation struggle. Not only that, but a definite affinity and preference towards specific cultural forms are displayed. This consistency of position and the forms preferred have not been peculiar to the current work only by Micere Mugo but have to be seen as continuities and developments from her preceding works.

In the Preface to *The Trial of Dedan Kimathi*, which she co-authored with Ngugi wa Thiong'o, she defines her conception of the function of the writer and theatre:

> African Literature and African Writers are either fighting with the people or aiding imperialism and the class enemies of the people. We believe that good theatre is that which is on the side of the people, that which, without masking mistakes and weaknesses, gives people courage and urges them to higher resolves in their struggle for total liberation.

The play goes on not only to endow Kimathi, the commander of the Mau Mau struggle, with a heroic stature but also situates him within the colonial and post-colonial struggles for economic and political liberation. It portrays Mau Mau as inevitable and not an aberration as some historians would have us believe. In it is an unequivocal political perspective that centres on the people as makers of history and thus agents of change within that history. Resistance against all factors that inhibit the people's capacity in the realization of their fullest potential as human beings and actors in history is one major factor for optimism in Africa's oppressive post-colonial reality. This is a perspective that we get in some of the poems in Micere Mugo's *Daughter of My People Sing*, a collection of poems written between 1966 and 1973 but published in 1976.

The poems of *Daughter of My People Sing!* touch upon many subjects — social relationships, human emotions, personal and communal experiences with nature, alienation and conflict. What stands out in this collection, however, are those poems which deal with issues of history, class differentiations, violence and the struggles that arise from these. This is typified by two of the longest poems in the collection — 'Up here, down there' and 'Vistas of Violent History'. While the first poem is developed around the contrasting images of the haves and have-nots as represented by the 'Wabenzi' with the mansions, 'cool groves with flower gardens' on the one hand, and the 'Kunguni Tele' (those full of ticks and parasitical vermin) in 'Dusty Barrenness', the second poem evokes a panorama of historical struggles with a Pan-African view point. Her concern for justice is expressed in such poems as 'Haki is Dead':

> I wish the rumour
> were not true
> that Haki is dead
> and buried
> that her hut
> was set on fire
> times ago
> animals saughtered
> children driven out
> from the small
> round hut
> they loved so well.

In this poem Mugo laments the absence of justice (*haki* in Kiswahili) and the consequent prevalence of human brutalities. More importantly, by posing the death of Haki as a rumour, the poem suggests the possibility of its being true open. Maybe Haki is critically sick and not dead yet? Chances of recovery exist. This optimism would be characteristic of Mugo's political stance regarding history and social change.

The political character of Mugo's poetry, however, comes of age with the poems in this current volume. The poems embody the author's lifelong concerns as writer and poet, woman, cultural and political activist. As a consequence, the youth, women and issues of gender, liberation struggles and resistance in a Pan-Africanist and Internationalist perspective form the backbone of the subject matter of the poems. The constricting and suffocating reality of the majority of the people in Africa and other parts of the world with the endless social injustices, political repressions and economic inequalities are presented in relentless, unambiguous images. These are given immediacy by drawing attention to the ongoing Pan-African and global struggles for justice, freedom, democracy and human rights in Mozambique, Angola, Ethiopia, Cuba, Somalia and the Americas, to name just a few. In spite of the vivid depiction of the brutal realities out of which these struggles arise, the total mood of the poems is not one of despair but of optimism. This optimism is situated in the possibility of political and economic liberation brought about by resistance and the collective will of the people.

The portrayal of the cruelty of oppression, imperialism, racism and apartheid, on the one hand, and the optimism and hope through resistance, on the other, are embodied in the very first poem in this volume, 'Birth'. Borrowing from Ayi Kwei Armah's *'The Beautyful Ones Are Not Yet Born'*, the author negates the despair and pessimism of Armah's novel by the counter proposition of 'the beautiful ones were born' in spite and because of 'The lowlands of despair' but amidst 'obstinate resistance and flowing river of momentous triumph'. They are carried through in 'The Isle of Youth' and 'In Praise of Africa's Children' which like 'Birth' focuses on the children and youth. In 'The Isle of Youth', America's oppressive economic measures against Cuba are counterpoised by an optimistic view of the future as represented by the youth who 'dive/into the deep waters/ and capture the sun'. Images of death depicting the plight of children who have been 'turned into living horrors' are followed by images of rebirth in 'In Praise of Afrika's Children'. Anger, dismay, frustrations and disillusionment in view of cultural crisis, independence, betrayals and institutionalized repressions are accompanied by expressions of defiance in 'On this Tenth Milestone', 'We Salute You', 'The Unknown Combatants Poem', 'We will Rise' and 'Build a Nation' and 'The Prosaic Poem'. If there is one prevailing value dominant in this volume it is that of a salute to the spirit of resistance.

The poems as a whole display also a conscious, high level of gender sensitivity and highlight women as actors in history. There is a dis-proportionate large number of poems which are salutes to unsung 'Matriots' (a word coined by the author and hopefully will stay in the English language) of Africana history and their resistance spirit. Invariably the poems call for international solidarity in women's struggles expressed in such poems as 'Mother Afrika's Matriots', 'The Woman's Poem', 'The Unknown Combatants', 'Plant a Tree' and 'My Mother's Poem'. In 'To be a Feminist', Mugo does not only provide the context of woman's struggles but also tackles one of the thorniest issues in contemporary discourse — feminism. The poem tries to revamp some notions of feminism propagated by some European/American scholars who assume a Eurocentric approach to issues of gender and class. At the same time, it negates the notion that feminism is not a concern for Africana women. For to be a feminist, the poem argues, is 'to unseat domination/and forge a rock out of powerlessness'. It is a thesis which ties women's struggles to others by dominated groups. The poem is, nevertheless, provocative and should contribute to the ongoing debate.

Included in 'Daughter of My People Sing!', was a poem entitled, 'Where are the Songs' in which the writer asked:

> Where are the songs
> my mother and yours sang
> always sang
> fitting rhythms
> to the whole
> vast span of life?

The question was posed at a time when discussions on forms and styles of African creative and literary output was picking up momentum. Three major trends were developing in which African writers opted for either following European poetic styles, adopting an African poetic or assimilating the two. Of those who tried to use African poetic forms, Okot p'Bitek stands out. His songs have generated controversial discussions without diminishing the importance of their pioneering contribution as a contemporary poetic genre. Mugo openly acknowledges the debt of inspiration she owes p'Bitek but has gone her own way in developing a style for her creative works. The present volume, therefore, displays continuity in search of a style. In this, she has gone a long way in answering her own question posed in the poem above by an intensive use of orature forms and characteristics.

Orature forms carry with them certain characteristics which

endow them with dynamism. These include ways of mediating reality based on keen observation and interpretation of phenomena, social and human activity, ingenuity of expressions, portrayal and imaginative manipulations. They are compositions which have a tradition of being sung, recited, spoken and performed for a variety of purposes. One of the often cited characteristics of orature is the relative absence of distance between audience and performers. This is because of the high level of participation inherent in most orature forms. The poems in this volume are, for the most part, structured as songs and the element of participation is quite obvious. The leader/chorus style in whih the audience is called upon to actively participate predominates.

The use of orature forms in contemporary African poetry has often highlighted a tension which is not always resolved. This is a tension between, on the one hand, the private and reflective mood of European poetic expression, which African writers have invariably been exposed to and most often adopt, and the obvious public expression of orature forms on the other. The public nature of orature resides in its performance element which is central to its effectiveness. The assimilation of orature in styles that contain and stifle its performance element is usually the source of the tension that can be seen in the works of some contemporary writers. The poems here display no such tension primarily because Mugo has structured them so that they demand dramatization and performance. One is made to feel that reading these poems individually and in private is not only undesirable but also that the exercise deducts essential elements necessary for their existence as poetic forms.

The way that imagery is used in the poems is another element of interest. The images used are given a vividness by the use of contrasts — soft/hard, closed/open, good/evil, life/death, liberation/oppression. As in other orature forms, the environment and natural phenomena are the major sources from which the images are drawn. Emphasis is achieved through an accumulation of images that strengthen each other. In one verse of 'Birth', for example, 'howling jackals', 'scavenging hyenas', 'stampeding elephants', 'pouncing wild tigers' and 'gulping ogres' reinforce each other as images of post-colonial repression. The combination of accumulated imagery and the often used refrains dictate a rhythm and pace which is both dramatic and uneven, characteristics which orature forms thrive on.

One can look at the use of orature in this volume to be consistent with the general political objectives of the writer. Orature forms have survived in Africa in spite of and because of colonialism. Because of the antagonism and repressions unleashed by colonialism against African people and their culture, to actively engage in cultural practice became an act of political resistance. It is due to this resistance that aspects of African cultural practices have survived. To use orature forms, therefore, is to simultaneously recognize their dynamism as cultural expressive forms and as a domain of resistance, historically. As pointed out earlier, the issue of resistance is one of the major areas celebrated and saluted in this volume.

This volume of poems is a welcome addition to the corpus of contemporary African creative production. One hopes that it will soon be found in translation in African languages, whose contribution to the aesthetics of the poems has endowed them with a uniqueness of their own.

Amandina Lihamba

Birth

For my daughters, Mumbi and Njeri
companions, friends and unfailing
comrades in the struggles, especially
during our mountainous life in exile.

Refrain: The Beautiful Ones Were Born

The beautiful ones
were born
> under leopard skies
> under roaring thunder
> under flooding rain
> under drowning earth

Refrain

The beautiful ones
were born
> before the grandeur
> of the majestic Rift Valley
> over Kilimanjaro in defiance
> Up Kirinyaga in awesome victory

Refrain

The beautiful ones
were born
> in the land of Me Katilili
> the home of Koitalel arap Samoei
> on the soil of Muthoni wa Kirima
> the birthright of Kimathi wa Wachiuri

Refrain

The beautiful ones
were born

1

over the spoils of Karen Blixen
along the horse tracks of De la Mere
above the adventures of Elspeth Huxley
amidst the bullets of colonial guns

Refrain

The beautiful ones
were born

in the human jungles
of neo-colonial treachery
under person-eat-person
development economics

Refrain

The beautiful ones
were born

amidst howling jackals
and scavenging hyenas
under stampeding elephants
and pouncing wild tigers
inside the mouths of gulping ogres

Refrain

The beautiful ones
were born

through hours of pain
in the heat of battle
at the heart of the struggle
under the blinding bulbs
of interrogating chambers

Refrain

The beautiful ones
were born

against chilling winds
under the scorching sun
amidst hunger and drought
around cries of piercing agony
through dehumanization and death

Refrain

The beautiful ones
were born

in the lowlands of despair
through valleys of elusive hope
across ridges of obstinate resistance
on the highlands of mounting optimism
by the flowing rivers of momentous triumph
aboard growing visions of internationalist victor

Refrain

In Praise of Afrika's Children

*For the children of Mozambique
and all Afrikana children who
have been orphaned biologically,
socially, politically, economically*

Refrain: I want to Sing

I want to sing
                    a love song
A song exploding
                    with feeling
A song blossoming
                    with beauty
like the flowering bud
unfolding wide
to embrace the rays
of the inviting sun.

Refrain

I want to sing
                    a love song
A song for
            my little
            tender ones
A song in praise of
                    my loved ones
from Cape to Cairo
from the sunrise
to sunset
A love song
            for my babies
            cremated
            and buried
            before their birth

4

I want to sing
                a love song
A song for
           my little
           tender ones
A song in praise of
                my loved ones
scattered by imperialist
                    history
across the Americas
across the Caribbean
Piled up in
           global mass graves
           etched shallow
           under ocean depths
across the length
and breadth
of Western history's
                  murderous face
from Goree to Martinique
from Sao Tome to Brazil
From Takoradi to Carolina.

Melodies of love
                well within me
Rivers of love
          flow through
          my heart
Torrents of passion
              flood my veins
I am full to overflowing.

But what song
shall I sing?

What song
shall I sing
        without mocking
        what I would praise?
What poem
shall I compose
in praise of
        skeleton shapes
        that desperately tug
        my dangling breast
        long drained
        of the last
        drop
        of milk?
What song
shall I sing?

Refrain

What words
shall I utter
in praise of
        ghostly shadows
        that populate
        the wasteland
        that Mother Africa is
in its Somalias
in its Mozambiques?
What song
shall I sing?

Refrain

What language
shall I fashion
in praise of

half beings
garbage-piled
sausage style
in sprawling ghettoes
from Harlem to Soweto
from Lagos to Brighton
from Mathare Valley to Rio
From Kinshasa to Marseille?

What language
shall I fashion?
Oh, what song
shall I sing?

Refrain

What poem
shall I compose
in praise of
decomposing human remains
mutilated human corpses
walking human skeletons
haunting our Mozambiques?
Caricatures of
human form
violated beings
exhibiting
pruned ears
dug-out eyes
butchered noses
chopped-off hands
sawed-off legs?
What poem
shall I compose?
What song
shall I sing?

What poem
shall I compose
in praise of
              human remains
              crippled lives
              walking corpses
Afrika's children
turned
              into living horrors
Afrika's children
crushed
              into shapelessness
mashed
              into formlessness
by Apartheid-Renamo machetes
America's anti-communist dollars?
What poem
shall I compose?
Oh, what song
shall I sing?

Refrain

What dance
shall I dance
in celebration of
                   chunks and stumps
                   that once held arms
                   suspended trunks
                   that once carried legs
                   gaping holes
                   that once encased eyes
                   jeering teeth
                   that once knew lips
                   shattered hearts
                   that once pulsated
                   with life?

8

What dance
shall I dance?
Oh, what song
shall I sing?

Refrain

What song
shall I sing
in praise of
            our children
living in
the mass graves
            of apartheid
            of capitalism
            of imperialism?
What song
shall I sing?

Refrain

I will sing
        a war song
My words
will be
        angry bullets
from the
        volcanic barrel
        of the well-aimed
        AK rifle
        of my poem
Each furious shot
                the staccato thunder
                of the well-measured
                machine gun
                of my actions
Each telling victory
                the raised salute
                of the never-dying

                              people's will
                              people's vision
detonating
                    racism
                    apartheid
                    imperialism
                    and their warlords.

And then
I will sing

Refrain

I will sing
                    a love song
A song
                    exploded with feeling
A song
                    bursting with laughter
A song
                    flowering with beauty
A song
                    caressing with tenderness
A song
                    embalmed with sweetness
A song
                    soothing with comfort
A song
                    for my innocent
                    tender ones
A song
                    in praise
                    of my loved ones
A song
                    in ululation
                    of my brave ones
from the Cape to Cairo
from Mombasa to Takoradi

from New York to San Francisco
from Trinidad to Belize
from Nova Scotia to Vancouver
from Brazil to Grenada

Refrain

Oh, I will sing
a song
I will sing
a love song
          a love song
          for my children
          a love song
          for my loved ones
          a love song
          for my babies
reborn
     through thunder
reborn
     through pain
reborn
     through death
reborn
     through vision
reborn
     through love.

Refrain–twice over.

Priscilla

Composed for the Zambuko/Izibuko theatre group's ngonjera *at the ZACT cultural centre in memory of Priscilla Maponga who had just passed away, May 1991.*

Watching
            the disappearing rays
of the setting sun
                        of Ghana's *uhuru*
the artist's pen
                        caught the twilight
                        of the retiring sun
composing
            a funeral dirge:
The Beautyful Ones
Are Not Yet Born!

Three decades after
Priscilla Maponga died
Priscilla Maponga
                        of Zambuko/Izibuko
                        community theatre family
Dipuo Mkhize
            of *Mandela —Spirit of No Surrender*
Dipuo Mkhize
            of the Soweto Youth Uprising
Dipuo Mkhize
            my enshrined theatre sister
Dipuo Mkhize
Priscilla Maponga
                        who lives on
                        long after sunset.

In undying memory
of the bright morning
                        that your life

                                    shall always
                                    be
We, Zambuko/Izibuko
                                    creators
                                    workers
invoke your name.

We, Zambuko/Izibuko
                                    cultural workers
                                    compose a text
                                    bridging the ford
                                    between you and us
                                    celebrating you
                                    as our soloist
                                    as our star.
In chorus
            and echoing volume
we sing
        and dance
choreographing
                    our statement
through rounded rhythms.

Our Priscilla
                    is the moon
                    that smiles
                    through the clouds
Our Dipuo
            is the ray
            that emerges
            through an eclipse.
Dipuo Mkhize
                    of the children's uprising
Dipuo Mkhize
                    of the Soweto Massacres
Dipuo Mkhize
                    of the spirit

of no surrender
                    which we poetize
                    with our voices
                    which we poetize
                    with our feet
                    which we poetize
                    with our action.

In echoing volume
chokwadi we say:

Priscilla Maponga
                    you were born
The beautiful ones
                    were born
                    have been born
                    are being born
                    will be born

One Priscilla
            two Priscillas
                        ten Priscillas
                                    Priscillas upon
                                    Priscillas
                                            upon
generations of Priscillas
whose living spirit
and creative beauty
no death can touch.

The Isle of Youth

*In memory of the most striking image
of my visit to Cuba: its vigorous youth
and their infectious optimism for a
future interlaced with avenues of hope*

On the Isle of Youth
I sat in the sun
                    of hope
I absorbed the sunshine
                            of optimism
as it streamed through
                        the seeing eyes
                        and speaking voices
of Cuba's youth.

I was warmed
                by the rays
                of their joyfulness
I was touched
                by the tenor
                of their laughter
I was captured
                by the magic
                of their dreams.

On the Isle of Youth
I watched
            America's economic blockade
            helplessly float on the sea waters
            of the undaunted Caribbean
I witnessed
            the youth dance
            in celebration
            on the dry shores

I saw the sun

       plunge
       into the deep waters

I saw the youth

       dive
       into the deep waters
       and capture the sun.

I smiled

     as they surfaced
     holding onto the beams

I marvelled

      as they perched it
      back onto the sky

I lay on my back

       gazing at the sun
       absorbing the sunshine
       of revolutionary visions.

A Healing Moment

For all global youth committed to
the struggle for human justice

The e is laughter
in my bloodstream
and massaging healing
in my veins
whenever I am
in contact
with any touching
human encounter.

There is no moment
so triumphant
as when
my heart touches
a small patch
of a human
liberated zone.

I drink
the feelings
of an intensely lived
eternal moment
which flashes past
but lives on
inside me
for ever.

I have feasted upon
sustaining human moments
I have hugged
rich and enriching
passing, yet eternal
human touches

To-night I have
                    communed with
intimate *untu*
                    healing contact
                    reaching dialogue
To-night I have
                    been lifted
by a human touch.

It is an evening of
unthawing the silences
releasing those voices
perpetually trapped
in the dwarfing metaphors
and the engulfing symbols
of stifling existence.

It is an evening of
naming oppression
through poetry
in the orature tradition.

When the applause
exhausts itself
a young man emerges
through a tellingly
correct but warm
foreign audience . . .

A suspended moment
hangs between us.

I stretch out
my feelings
                    and my hand
in readiness
                    for a handtouch

The young man
reaches out
           with open arms
and touches me
with his
           authentic words:

"May I please ask…"
(then comes the question)
"…for a hug?"

In these human winter times
hot with new world order myths
In these cold dollar days
abundant with rationed human feelings
the already answered question
gives birth to the mother in me.

I am reminded that
another woman's son
is my child
that my sister's baby
is my baby
that my daughter
is your child
that all the world's children
are my children
— our children.

Intellectuals or Imposters?

Refrain: Aha! Intellectuals or imposters?

When problems
                translate into
                deep seas
deep seas
daring
                philosophical diving
deep seas
daring
            skills in
            floating
            swimming
            surfacing
show me those
who emerge
                treading water
                walking the shores
                breathing courage
                and conviction
                scanning the horizon
a horizon extended
                unto eternity
an eternity
            of enquiry.
Show me those
who cast
            a penetrating eye
disentangling
                a maze of problems
                defying all solution.
Show me these
and I will tell you
                whether they are
                intellectuals
                or imposters.

Show me those

       who walk the shore
       firming the earth
       on which
       we stand
       shaping up visions

visions that
clearly define

       who they are
       whom we are
       where we are
       when we are
       how we are
       how to be.

Yes, show me these
and I will tell you

       whether they are
       intellectuals
       or imposters.

Refrain

Show me those
who cross

       engulfing seas
       seas of confusion

those who build

       connecting bridges
       bridges of understanding

those who traverse

       dividing gorges
       gorges of alienation.

Show me those
who leap-frog

       with human grace

hurdles of
            ego-tripping.
Friend, show me these
and I will tell you
                Whether they are
                intellectuals
                or imposters.

Refrain

Show me those
who break
                icicles
                of silences
those who untie
                stammering tongues
those who teach
                articulation
articulation of
                the aunthentic word.
Show me these
and I will tell you
                who are the intellectuals
                and who are the imposters.

Refrain

Tell me too
tell me
                where they stand
                whether on the soil
                of liberating knowledge
                or upon the sands
                of unfounded learning.
Tell me
tell me whether
                they surround the furnace
                of living wisdom

that generates the heat
of probing dialogue
and teasing ideas.
Tell me this
and I will tell you
how I know them
how I see them
where I place them.

Refrain

Tell me
tell me
whether they stand
to the north
to the south
to the west
or to the east
of the compass
of our people's lives.
Tell me this
and I will tell you
where they are
coming from
and where they may be
headed to.
Yes, tell me this
and I will tell you
whether they are
intellectuals
or imposters.

Refrain

Draw me
the circumference
of the circle
that surrounds them

23

Show me
              where they have
              positioned
              themselves
                        whether they be
                                        at the center
              or on the periphery
of pro-people
              human rights debate.
Draw me
this circle
and I will tell you
                        whether they truly stand
                        or decorate the fence
                        of abdicating neutrality.
Friend, tell me this
and I will tell you
                        whether they are
                        intellectuals
                        or imposters.

Refrain

Capture me
capture me
              the podium
the podium
from which
              they deliver
              their treatises
              of academia
              whether they deposit
              engulfing piles
              of alienating information
              or micro-examine facts
              through the mirror
              of reflected
              and tested reality

Yes, capture me
                the scene
and I will tell you
                whether they are
                intellectuals
                or imposters.

Refrain

Capture me
capture me
                this grandiose scene
                of academia
                with its dons
                and their wisdom
Capture me
                the scene
and I will tell you
                whether the missiles
                of their ideas
                hit the target
                or bounce back
                on an overlooking
                blank stone wall
                Of incomprehension
Friend, capture me
                the scene
and I will tell you
                whether they are
                intellectuals
                or imposters.

Refrain

Tell me
tell me
          whether they are
          perched

25

statue-like
on the high chairs
of bureaucratic
stuffiness
pushing heaps
of reluctant paperwork
heaps that solidify
into immovable boulders
sitting on forbidding
mountains
of accumulated
red tap
Tell me this
and I will tell you
why they bake
themselves
in stuffy Anglo-American
and Franco-German suits
in the heat
of Africa's problems.
Yes, I will tell you
why the madams
choke themselves
with chains of gold
around sagging necks
while our children
writhe with the agony
of crippling hunger
and the diarrhoea
of malnutrition

Friend, tell me this
and I will tell you
whether they are
intellectuals
or imposters.

tell me whether
                they penetrate
                the forests of intrigue
                and bushes of lies
                planted by
                stampeding
                political elephants
                and buffaloes
                who mercilessly crush
                our people's lives
                under their hoofs
                making minced meat
                of their lives
Yes, tell me whether
                    the reels of theories
                    they abstractly kite-fly
                    remain suspended in the sky
                    or make a landing
                    on people's earth
whether they sit
                solitarily confined
                inside the cells
                of incarcerating
                academia
or whether they flower
                        like ripened plants
                        bearing the seeds
                        of education for living
Yes, tell me this
and I will tell you
                whether they are
                intellectuals
                or imposters.

Tell me
tell me whether

               their theories are
               active volcanoes
               erupting with
               fertilizing lava
               on which to plant
               seeds that will
               germinate
               with self-knowledge
               seeds that will
               cross-fertilize
               into collective being
Knowledge become
               actioned theory
Knowledge become
               living testimony
               of our people's
               affirmative history
               liberated *herstory*
Actioned theory
               inscribed as·
               a protest
               manifesto
               re-aligning our people's
               averted humanity
Yes, tell me this
and I will tell you
               whether they are
               intellectuals
               or imposters.

Refrain

Mother Afrika's Matriots

*A contribution towards the urgent task
of engendering Pan-Africanism, our
historical memories, our language and
concepts such as "patriots" etc. etc.*

Refrain: Mother Afrika's Matriots

When we surmount
                          an attack
on the unfinished
                          business
of historical stock-taking
we shall begin
with dynamizing
                          freezing silences
                          now paralyzing
our womanful lives.

We shall recount
                          our herstory
dramatizing it
and illustrating it
with rainbow colours.

We will pour lavish
                          libation
                          honouring
named
un-namable
yet to be named
Mother Afrika's matriots.

Refrain

We will sing
                without counting time
We will dance
                hearts touching earth
We will map
                the A and the Z
of our unfolding
epic journey
                of womanful living
We will compose
                immortal verse
in living praise of
Mother Afrika's matriots.

Refrain

Nefertiti, the ever poised gazelle
legendary beauty, granary of culture
whose stunning reign rained sparkling stars.

Refrain

Hatshepsut, grand political architect
who artfully engraved plateaus
of human development while Europe still slept.

Refrain

Cleopatra, commanderess of matriotic forces
strategist of unfathomable battlecraft
whose stature not even William can shake or spear.

Refrain

Anne Nzinga, proud, stately daughter of the Matamba
unconquered queen of Ndongo, abolitionist supreme
who etched liberation anthems across Angola's valleys and
hills.

30

Refrain

Harriet Tubman, orature artist from Afrika's health
uncaptured guerilla of the underground railroad
whose untiring feet carved corridors of freedom south to
north.

Refrain

Jane Lewis, detonator of America's dungeons of slavery
who engineered highways across Ohio's angry waters
navigating slave rescue boats under the enslaver's jaundiced
eye.

Refrain

Mary Prince, fearless daughter of sustaining Afrikan soil
who spat on the virulent crumb-eating housenigger cult
burning with each stroke of her pen Caribbea's slave-ridden
fields.

Refrain

Mary Seacole, Afrikan of undying Jamaican maroon seed
whose womanful vision uncovered all male chilvarly myths
urging sisters to pilot their herstory to newly aimed heights.

Refrain

Gertrude Gomez de Avellanda of defiant, revolutionary Cuba
who composed a resounding feminist choral poem ages gone
since highjacked by plagiarizers and forgers of the feminist
text.

Refrain

Sojourner Truth, earthquake that shook pillars of racism and
    sexism —

Mary C. Terrell, educator, life-long campaigner for women's
    rights —
Ida B. Wells, journalist-activist, source of liberating
    consciousness —

Refrain

Frances Harper, poetess and orator of melodious anti-slavery
    tunes —
Lucy Parson, unsetting sun on black working class life of
    struggle —
Ella Baker, weaver of grassroots networks for civil rights
    activism —

Refrain

Fannie Iou Hamer, resister before whose vision Mississippi
    trembled —
Audrey Jeffers, clarion for Afrikana sisters to combat racial
    assault —
Amy Ashwood Garvey, Pan-Africanist feminist who
    unchained wifewood —

Refrain

Mary McLeod Bethune, heartbeat of Afrikan war drums for
    freedom —
Clara McBride, "Mother Hale", utmost symbol of Afrikana
    motherhood —
Queen Mother Moore, Audley of Louisiana, spine of Afrikana
    struggles —

Refrain

Women valiants, whose fighting spirit was a mighty wall of
defence —
surrounding Afrika, stretching defiantly east to west, north to
south —

Yaa Asantewa, Mihayra Bint Aboud, Queen Aminata,
Mamfengu, Ma Rarabe —

Refrain

Sisters who took over guard, fortifying the wall with gallant
    resistance —
Nyakasikana Mbuya Nehanda of the undying Munhumutapa
    fighting stock —
Me Katilili wa Menza, daughter of Kenya, orator, mobilizer
    unsurpassed —

Refrain

Rosa Parks, whose enthroned dignity no racist bigot could
    unseat —
Mary Muthoni Nyanjiru who reignited a retreating volcano of
    workers —
Muthoni wa Kirima, last fieldmarshall of the Mau Mau
    landfreedom army —

Refrain

Mother Afrika's matriots will rise the earthshaking power of:
the Aba women
the Abeokuta women
the Maji Maji women
and the *jua kali* women

They will rise with the roaring fury of:
the Dakar railway strike women
the Defiance Campaign women
and the Black Panther women

They will rise with the sweeping force
of Mother Afrika's struggling women
Our matriots will surely rise
with the gun salute
                    of the final *chimurenga*

33

picking up the molotovs
                              that missed the target
last *chimurenga* around
aiming with the precision of
Afrikana *chimurenga* women of:

Haiti and Cuba
Algeria and Kenya
Mozambique and Angola
Guinea Bissau and Namibia
Zimbabwe and South Afrika.

They will explode imperialist history's
                                   incarcerating myths
They will light undying flames
                              of liberating visions
They will accurately shape
                              the A and the Z
of our unfolding pilgrimage
through herstory
through living
through being.

                    Refrain

When we surmount
                         an attack
on the unfinished
                         business
of historical stock-taking
we shall begin
with dynamizing
                    freezing silences
                    now paralyzing
our womanful lives.

We shall recount
                    herstory

34

dramatizing it
and illustrating it
with rainbow colours.

We will pour lavish
                    libation
                    honouring
named
un-namable
yet to be named
Mother Afrika's matriots.

We will sing
                    without counting time
We will dance
                    hearts touching earth
We will feast
                    on nourishing visions
nourishing visions
of womanful living
through womanful
                    herstory.

We will map
                    the A and the Z
of our unfolding
epic journey
                    of womanful struggles

We will compose
                    immortal verse
in living praise of
Mother Afrika's matriots.

                    Refrain

To be a Feminist is

In an effort to liberate the concept of feminism from abduction by Western bourgeois appropriators and in the spirit of naming the essence, rather than simply peeling off the label.

Refrain: To be a Feminist is

For me
to be a feminist is

>   to embrace my womanness
>   the womanness of
>   all my mothers
>   all my sisters
>   it is
>   to hug the female principle
>   and the metaphors of life
>   that decorate my being

Refrain

For me
to be a feminist is

>   to celebrate my birth
>   as a girl
>   to ululate that my gender
>   is female
>   it is
>   to make contact
>   with my being.

Refrain

For me
to be a feminist is

>   to denounce patriarchy
>   and the caging of women

           it is
           to wipe the fuzziness
           of colonial hangovers
           to uproot the weeds
           of neo-colonial pestilence

Refrain

For me
to be a feminist is
                    to hurl
                    through the cannon
                    of my exploding
                    righteous fury
                    the cannibal
                    named capitalism
                    it is
                    to pronounce
                    a death sentence
                    on the ogre
                    named imperialism.

Refrain

For me
to be a feminist is
                    to unhood racism
                    to decry zionism
                    to detonate apartheid
                    to obliterate "tribalism"
                    it is
                    to necklace homophobia
                    to drown fanaticism
                    to strangulate classism
                    to fumigate ethnic cleansing.

Refrain

For me
to be a feminist is

> to speak out loud
> to articulate my name
> to assert that I am
> to declare that woman is
> it is
> to water my fertility
> to woman my womb
> it is
> to converse with my soul.

Refrain

For me
to be a feminist is

> to burst all the non-space
> between the bedroom
> and the kitchen
> of my life
> it is
> to grow wings
> and fly
> to unlimited heights
> it is
> to ride the sun
> of my visions.

Refrain

For me
to be a feminist is

> to celebrate my mother
> to poetize my sisters
> to message their failures
> it is
> to savour their intellect
> to drink their feelings

and to embrace
their achievements.

Refrain

For me
to be a feminist is

        to curdle my children's hopes
        to infuse their veins
        with the spirit
        of never-say-die
        it is
        to fan their wind
        of resistance
        to stroke them
        with optimism
        it is
        to give them
        to humanity.

Refrain

For me
to be a feminist is

        to have dialogue
        with my father
        and my brother
        to invite their partnership
        as fellow guerillas
        it is
        to march with them
        to the war-torn zone
        of Afrikana survival
        it is
        to jointly raise with them
        the victory salute.

Refrain

For me
to be a feminist is

> to part ways
> with the bulging haves
> to merge paths
> with the stricken have-nots
> it is
> to know that
> deprivation consumes
> it is
> to see that
> overeating constipates
> it is
> to level mountains
> of obnoxious accumulation
> it is
> to rain upon deserts
> of annihilating nothingness.

Refrain

For me
to be a feminist is

> to breathe the air
> of unpolluted peoplehood
> and to sing
> in harmony with nature
> it is
> to touch
> the soft earth
> it is
> to speak
> with the unknown
> it is
> to walk this life
> it is
> to hold up the sky.

Refrain

40

For me
to be a feminist is

                to unseat domination
                and forge a rock
                out of powerlessness
                it is
                to shake hands
                with people's struggles
                it is
                to disempower
                superpower arrogance
                it is
                to conceive and deliver
                a human world.

Refrain

For me
to be a feminist is

                to be me
                an Afrikan woman
                all Afrikana women
                and all who have walked
                their path of thorns
                it is
                to know herstory
                word for word
                it is
                to look history
                in the face
                and declare
                that I am
                because woman is.

Refrain

For me
to be a feminist is

                to be the mother

41

of my daughters
it is
to be the daughter
of my mother
it is
to be more than
a survivor
it is
to be a creator
it is
to be a woman.

Refrain

The Woman's Poem

The refrain is a Gikuyu and English
mixed grill/hybrid for "just imagine!"

Refrain: Ta Imaaaagini!

Ta imagini that
you and I
and all the women
of this world
stood hand in hand
marched side by side
                    crossing
                              dividing borders
                    constructing
                                   connecting bridges
                    shattering
                              binding chains
                    creating
                              delinkable links
across the nations
across the continents!

Refrain

Ta imagini that
all the multitude
of pro-women forces
stood hand in hand
marched side by side
forming
          one mighty waterfall
          of sweeping
          human masswaters
          flooding and drowning
          into the ocean

43

all forms of oppression!

Refrain

Ta imagini that
our wombs
        issued forth
                one populous
                        global family
                                of women
                                        combatants

building a ladder
to step up the struggle
founding a wall
to firm up resistance
resting on shoulders
of reckoning victory!

Refrain

Ta imagini that
our hearts
        were merged
and that
our minds
        were fused
in composing
        one eternal
                        creation poem
in enacting
        one non-ending
                        feminist drama!

Refrain

Ta imagini that
this theatre starred

44

                    one mammoth
                                    sea of women
so mobilized
                no one can rip off
a force
so militant
                no patriarchy can molest
a family
so united
                no racism can separate
a human breed
so liberated
                no classism can divide!

Refrain

Ta imagini that
we exploded
                chilling silences
defrosted
                refrigerated womanhood
pestled and mortared
                        the chains
                        that grate
                        and grind us!

Refrain

Ta imagini that
we blasted
                self-effacement
question-marked
                our invisibility
hugged our
                irrepressible specialness
celebrated
                our stunning beautifulness

45

reclaimed
our ignored indispensability!

Refrain

Ta imagini that
we rolled
all those boulders
that blockade
our march forward
and that we moved
all the mountains
that obstruct
our vision onward
and that we penetrated
the thickets of myths
that capture and cage
our humanity
our womanhood!

Refrain

Ta imagini that
we freed
our hands
unbound
our feet
unfettered
our minds
liberated
our lives
piloting
our own
history
forward
forward
forward
advancing

                    advancing
                    advancing!

Refrain

Ta imagini that
we stripped
                    patriarchy naked
shouted
            foul to domination
thundered
                no to oppression
screamed
                murder to abuse
pronounced
                death to imperialism

declared
            war on classism!

Refrain

Ta imagini that
we painted
                    a limitless canvas of love
choreographed
                    a dance to empowerment
celebrated
                life for development
delivered
                true birth through woman
ululated
                ultimate growth in humankind!

Prolonged refrain

47

The Pan-Afrikanist Poem

For all those who struggle(d)
to establish Afrikana Studies on
campuses of cultural domination.
(Originally composed for the
50th birthday of brother J. Turner)

Comrade
when you picked up
                        your excavation tools
hoisting the hoe
                  on your shoulders
taking measured
                  determined strides
                  to the grave side
                  of our buried
                  Pan-Afrikanist
                  heritage
you dug up
a buried piece
of our family land.

You reclaimed
our piece
of buried land
soil overwhelmed
                        by poisonous weeds
                        life molestation
                        colonial violation
                        imperialist infestation
piece of land
                  ambushed by
                  western civilization
forested by
                  deception
                  and intrigue.

Comrade
you then
picked up
            your sharpened axe
and expertly felled
                        those dwarfing
                        giant trees
building with them
                        connecting bridges
                        from Mother Afrika
                        across the Middle Passage
linking
        divided landmasses and seas
                                linking us with us
                                herstory with history

Comrade
when you
            took hold of the dynamite
            and strategically exploded
            the invaders' fortified castles
            founded on historical lies,
me
your sister
balanced on
            my level head
a *makuti* basket
skillfully crafted
a *makuti* basket
            heaving with
            luscious fruit.

My head high
each footstep
etching a permanent
                sisterly presence
                on our reclaimed

                              patch
                              of Pan-African soil
I stood
          arrow-straight
on Afrikana Studies
                              land,
I stood
          expectantly pregnant
          with Afrikana dreams.

Looking deep
into your calm
                    Afrikana face
I poetized
for you
          and for myself
I poetized
for him
          and for her
I poetized
          for our children
          and for all of us
saying:
Comrade
we greet you!

On This Tenth Milestone

*For John La Rose of Beacon Books
on the 10th Anniversary of
the Black World Book Fair.*

Refrain: On this milestone

On this tenth milestone
                    of our steep ascent
along the mountainous path
                    of self-definition
we shall curve
            a comma
we shall observe
            a pause
we shall carpenter
            a springboard
then launch
        an accurate leap forward
aimed at
        the full stop and
        the exclamation mark
of our final statement.

Refrain

On this tenth milestone
                    of our steep ascent
along the mountainous path
                    of self-definition
we shall bake
        no birthday cake
we shall light
        no waxen candle
we shall decorate
        no festival hall

we shall build
                    a furious fire.

Refrain

Searching through
                    Mother Afrika'
                    forested hills
we shall liberate
                    the choicest wood
we shall build
                    a roaring fire
we shall encircle
                    the furious fire
we shall catch
                    its dancing flames
make them sing
                    our dancing song
make them dance
                    our dancing dance.

Refrain

Holding each other
                    warmth between us
hearing each other
                    barriers behind us
we shall regroup
                    for the final ascent
up the steep path
                    of self-definition
we shall delink
                    one by one
                    every link of
                    those gripping chains
we shall relink
                    all the rings
                    of our broken

            Afrikana
            family chain.

Refrain

Holding each other
                warmth between us
hearing each other
                barriers behind us
our unfettered minds
                shall freely glean
                the dry fields
                of a weed-infested
                history of famine
which we now punctuate
                with a bounteous
                harvest
on this our tenth year
                of tears and laughter
                silence and speech
                death and life.

Refrain

Holding each other
                warmth between us
hearing each other
                barriers behind us
our featherweight feet
                shall stage a dance
                in combat step
Combat dance
            telling the story
of a fighter
            holding ground
            ever defending
            human rights
Combat dance

unfolding the legend
of an activist
delivering blows
to racial injustice
Combat dance
in rhythm with
a champion
of popular culture
Combat dance
in conversation with
a militant
armed
with people's power
Combat dance
in image with
history's mirror
radiating
a myriad colours
of world masses
in global struggles.

Refrain

On this tenth milestone
of our steep ascent
along the mountainous path
of self-definition
we shall build
a furious fire
sing a song
heartbeat apace
with a comrade
A comrade born
under dispersal
in Trinidad
A comrade holding
the wild bull

54

of colonial oppression
by the horns
counselling bees
of labouring workers
to stop making honey
and learn how to sting.

Refrain

We shall build
a roaring fire
write the poem
of a freedom fighter
in Venezuela
cutting the chords
of enslaving culture
with razor-sharp vision
schooling the captives
to cease being parrots
and originate the word.

Refrain

We shall build
a furious fire
perfect a dance
for a comrade in arms
child of Trinidad
migrant to London
dismantling the traps
of abducting education
and throttling culture
reminding survivors
that breathing is politics
and learning, combat.

Refrain

On this our tenth year
                    of pain and pleasure
                    suffering and joy
                    tears and laughter
                    silence and song
                    death and life
                    celebration and vigilance
we shall build
                    a furious fire
we shall surround
                    the roaring fire
tell the legend
                    of a compatriot
child of Trinidad
mobilizer for Kenya
                    dislodging the clutches
                    of preying economics
                    dispersing auctioneers
                    of the air people breathe
reminding the vultures
                    a volcano erupts
                    a time-bomb explodes.

Refrain

On this tenth milestone
                    of our steep ascent
along the mountainous path
                    of self-definition
we shall bake
                    no birthday cake
we shall light
                    no waxen candles
we shall decorate
                    no festival hall
we shall build
                    a roaring fire

we shall encircle
                    the furious fire
we shall catch
                    its dancing flames
we shall hoist them
                    high on a beacon
adorned with symbols
                    of Afrikana struggles
telling the world
                    we were always there
                    and shall always be here.

Refrain

On this tenth
                    milestone
of our steep climb
along the mountainous path
                    of self-definition
we shall carpenter
                    a solid springboard
we shall launch
                    an accurate leap
an accurate leap
arrowed forward
                    an accurate leap
aimed at
          the comma
          and the full stop
          No!
          The exclamation mark
          of our final
          and complete
          statement!

Refrain

We Salute You

*For the Afrikana leader who has
not betrayed our people's struggles
for survival and human dignity.*

In these vulture-ridden, cannibal times
when hawks menacingly circle around us
gentlemanned in Hollywood fashion suits
madammed in glittering Parisian gems
in these vulture-ridden, cannibal times
when
      bulging pockets
      bursting stomachs
      and puffing cheeks
mock the skeleton
              shapes
of walking human
              ghosts,
we salute you
      comrade of the slim stomach
we salute you
      combatant of the soil
we salute you
      child of mother Afrika!

In these days of the weeping sun
when the world soaks under tears of want,
in these days of the bleeding moon
when bloodsucking has become an honourable crime,
we salute you
      comrade of modest living
we salute you
      comrade of human rights
we salute you
      child of mother Afrika.

In these remote-controlled
                                video-war times
when unborn babies
                        are viciously
                        ripped out
                        of protecting
                        and nurturing
                        mothers' wombs
by butchers and mercenaries
                                roaming our lands
making proverbial owls
                        of Afrikana women,
we salute you
                people's gallant fighter
we salute you
                combatant of the soil
we salute you
                child of mother Afrika!

In these nightmare-infested
                                sleep-void days
when imperialist agents
                        apply the whip
overseeing our oppression
                                lash after lash,
in these nightmare-infested
                                sleep-void days
we salute you
                comrade of the struggle
we salute you
                combatant of the soil
we salute you
                child of mother Afrika.

In these humanity-vacuumed
                                development days
when snarling rabid hounds

                              go loose on us
blood-thirstily sniffing
                         our disparaged soil
dismembering our bodies
                         limb by limb,
we salute you
            comrade of the struggle
we salute you
            combatant of the soil
we salute you
            child of mother Afrika

In these heart-chilling
                  lie-ridden times
when praise singers abuse
                     their voices with falsehoods
piling heaps of
            intoxicating flattery
            upon swelling tyrants
degreeing killers
            in mockery of freedom
gowning captors
of history
         in mockery of achievement,
in these heart-chilling
                  lie-ridden times
when
       knowledge haters
       intellect jailors
       truth abductors
mock the proud standing walls
encasing liberating knowledge,
we salute you
            comrade of the books
we salute you
            combatant of the soil
we salute you
            child of mother Afrika

The Unknown Combatant's Poem

For South Afrika's freedom fighters and other
combatants of our motherland in whose honour
I lay this poem as my wreath, at the tomb
of the unknown soldier, wherever this may be
on Afrika's Hero/ine(s) Acres.

Unknown combatant
                    symbol of our struggle
                    flame of our fighting spirit!
From this side
            of apartheid's prison yard
            we too vouch:
            It will be
            our motherland
            or death!

Taunting images
                    mock our angry eyes
Oppressive symbols
                    suffocate the life in us
Manacles of heavy iron
                    root our feet to the ground
Fetters of crushing chains
                    bind our bodies in captivity
Scorching anger
                burns our hearts
                corroding in its acidity.

But the soul
        of the being in us
remains
untouched
unmoved
unbent
obstinate
grounded
as a rock!

A stone ridge
              lashed upon
              by surging seawaves
              which retreat
                          scattered
                                  shattered
                                          spent
leaving the rock
              standing
              defiant
              unbroken
              unbreakable.

Haunting images
                mock our angry eyes
Skeleton shapes
              of abused
              mother Afrika's children
                              born
                              unborn
                              stillborn
                              locked in orphanage
lacerate our vision
                with blinding pain
The knifing images
                brutally tear
the innermost tissues
                of our hearts
But the soul
              of the being in us
remains
untouched
unnerved
unbroken
unbreakable!

 And the heartbeat
              of the being in us

remains
pulsating
with life
pumping fresh streams of blood
                              into our veins
pregnating our imagination
                        with creative visions
igniting our hearts
                  with fire and fury.

The being in us
is haunted
by the Sowetos
                  of our people's ghettoization
the Bantustans
                  of our people's marginalization
the Robben Islands
                    of our people's incarceration
the Sharpevilles
                  of our people's extermination.
The being in us
is choking
              in the smoke
              of industrial apartheid
crushing
          under the pits
          of apartheid goldmines
bleeding
            from lashes
            of apartheid sjamboks.
The being in us
is clawed
          by ugly
          clutching
          venomous
          apartheid
          fangs.

But the unconquerable
                    human being in us
will grenade
to smithereens
these nailing fangs
making out of them
fine powder
moulding
from the ashes
              the people's
              victory salute!
Affirmative
the human being in us will
freedom charter
                    our nation's wealth
freedom charter
                    our people's lives
freedom charter
                    our children's future!
Comrade combatant
                    symbol of our struggle
                    flame of our fighting spirit
we shall fight
we shall fight
till we stand
on both feet
              heirs and heiresses
              of our stolen birthright.
Affirmative
we too vouch:
              It will be
              our motherland
              or death!

A Question to Opposition Leaders

Refrain: How could you?

How could you
                crumble an agenda so long
                        an agenda
                        so painfully drawn
                        an agenda
                        written with the people's
                        sweat, blood and tears?

How could you?

How could you
                shrivel an agenda so alive
                        an agenda
                        so collectively assembled
                        shrinking it into a single
                        egoistic, trashable item:
                        state-house occupancy?

How could you?

How could you
                licence hunting finger cutters
                to chop people's votes
                while you musical chaired
                your state-house ambitions
                sitting on the laps of our struggles
                sinking the platform of our demands?

How could you?

How could you
                abort our democratic manifesto
                miscarrying an entrusted mandate
                while camel-loaded with oppression
                the masses roast like ants
                on the burning charcoals
                of hunger, poverty and dispossession?

How could you?
How could you?
How *could* you?
How could *you?*
How?

We planted you firmly

> on the people's
> raised platform

We cemented the base

> with our unbreakable
> collective will

We invited you

> to come and launch
> the jump forward
> into the future
> of our collective
> realization

But you missed
the springboard

> flinging yourselves
> and all of us
> onto the concrete
> of verbal civil war
> and bruising duels

You missed
the obvious target

> dragging back
> onto our breaking backs
> the crushing boulder
> of ruthless repression
> even as we dislodged it.

How could you?
How could you?
How *could* you?
How could *you?*
How?

66

In the collective name

of our struggling millions,
mighter than your ego,
re-route your derailed
democracy-bound train.
Passengers are still aboard
ready for the protracted journey
preparing to assume the driver's seat
on the life-long pilgrimage
along the path of self-determination.

In the collective name
of our struggling millions:

Will you?

We will Rise and Build a Nation

In defiance of neo-colonial dictators,
reminding them that even the darkest
of nights breaks into daylight and
that their days are truly numbered!

At independence

          we garlanded our leaders
          with embracing hearts
               hearts

                    whose unbending
                    veins
                    had survived
                    the burning heat
                    of colonialism
                    and the blazing hell
                    of dehumanization.

At independence

          we celebrated our leaders
          with earnest minds
               minds

                    whose flaming
                    imagination
                    had withstood
                    scalding years
                    of psychological
                    warfare
                    emerging whole
                    but with telling scars.

At independence

          we embraced our leaders
          with trusting hearts
               hearts

                    they soon shredded
                    flinging the tatters

                                        to the winds of
                                        betrayal
                                        auctioneering our faith
                                        in the cut-throat
                                        markets
                                        of transnational
                                        business.

At independence

                        we craftily wove together
                        the frayed hanging threads
                        of our fringe existence
                        making a monumental cloth
                        out of which we designed
                        our national liberation flag.

At independence

                        colonial collaborators snatched
                        our national liberation flag
                        highjacking our independence
                        with cunning serpentine imposture
                        twisting it into a rope
                        with which they strangulated our hopes
                        leaving us under neo-colonial barrenness.

Under neo-colonialism

                        anti-nationalists have mutilated
                        our national identity
                        massacred our national symbols
                        and buried them
                        under the primitive arithmetic
                        of ethnic subtraction and division.

Under neo-colonialism

                        our bodies are consumed
                        with keeping perpetual wakes
                        through nights of econo-political
                        funerals

Our nerves are wrenched
by persisting rending screams
from abused human rights victims.

Under neo-colonialism

our dignity is scattered like chaff
across the nothingness of peripheral
survival
our minds are terrorized with living
horrors
even as *Mworoto, Wagalla* and *Burnt
forest*
shoot poisoned ethnic cleansing
arrows
through the shields of justice and
liberty.

But we refuse

to leave our anger
scattered
on the wasteland
of our enemy's plunder

We swirl

with the sweeping fury
of a dust storm

We exhume

the graveyards
of our collective
conscience
levelling the tombs
of our destroyed nationhood
our assaulted peoplehood

We swirl

with the sweeping fury
of a dust storm

turning the graves
inside out
moulding from the remains
new women
new men
new youth.

To-morrow
We will rise
with the sweeping fury
of a dust storm
creating a new nation
ready to extinguish
the hell fire
of dictatorship.

We will blast
the iron bars
behind which
our children lie captive
We will convert
Kamiti prison
into a people's park
into our children's
playing field

We will fly home
exiled matriots
banished patriots
landing them home
on a newly built
Me Katilili Airport

We will plough
the barren fields
of our ravished
national economy
producing a surplus

of our full growth
and human potential

We will rise
and build a nation
moulding from the pieces
of an oppressive history
an unassailable monument
grafted with justice for all
enshrined with limitless hope.

Plant a Tree

*Poem composed for and recited at
a Tree Dedication Ceremony in honour
of Prof. Wangari Maathai and other
women in the Kenyan people's struggle,
Le Moyne College, June 24, 1992.*

On this abundant Le Moyne soil

>> nurturing trees
>> of unassailable knowledge

On this Onondaga native soil

> endowed birthright
> from immemorial dawn

On this bounteous Onondaga land

>> trampled upon
>> by Christ-opher Columbus
>> five hundred-burdened
>> years ago,

we who refuse
to stampede

> on humans
> soils or plant

Plant a tree!

A tree

> of resistance and struggle

A tree

> of justice and equality

A tree

> of dialogue and love

A tree

> so defiant
> of drought
> and plunder

than no human-made disaster
can shake it

73

A tree
        with roots
        anchored so deep
that no living destruction
can uproot it.

Side by side
        you and I
                will water
                        the seedling
                                till our tree
                                        is full- grown

till our tree
is forested
                with thickets
                of branches
                        stretching
                        reaching out
                South, North
                East, West
holding the leaves
                        to the sun
till in knowing
                rhythm
                they dance
                to the tune
of the humming wind
Till our tree
is forested
                with thickets
                of branches
                        stretching out
                        reaching out
beckoning to the birds
                        of the air
                        as they swim
                        across the sky

inviting the passing
                sky travellers
                to build nests
                make beds there
exhorting them
            to sing
            in high soprano
            songs of nature
entreating them
            to bathe
            in the wooing
            streaming rays
of the smiling sun.

Shoulder to shoulder
              you and I
                  will water
                        the tree of humanity
                                till full- grown
till its flowering
            stuns the world
            with loveliness
till natural beauty
            merges in fusion
            with human beauty
            till no child cries
                      tears of hurt
                      tears of hunger
till all Onondaga children
return from America's
              wild reservations
walking proud
on Onondaga
native land.

Hand in hand
            you and I
                will water

                              the tree
                              of sisterhood
                              and brotherhood
till the grown tree
            overwhelms the soil
            upon which division grows
and the grown tree
            will have
            a shade
            so encompassing
                              no heat wave
                              can touch it
            a shade
            so embracing
that unborn generations
shall shelter there
five hundred unborn years to come.

Five hundred unborn years to come
                              unborn generations
                              shall shelter there
unmolested by ogres
                  of imperialist greed.
Unborn generations
shall shelter there
playing
            in freedom
sleeping
            in peace
singing
            in triumph
            victorious songs
            from joyful
            overflowing hearts.

Unborn generations
shall shelter there

whispering
> healing words
> from tongue to tongue
> human voice to human voice.

Unborn generations
shall shelter there
basking
> under soothing calm

thriving
> under unconditional love

timelessly
> living
> being
> becoming.

On this abundant
> Le Moyne soil

nurturing trees
> of unassailable knowledge

On this Onondaga
> native soil

birthright
> from immemorial dawn

we who refuse
> to stampede
> on humans
> soil, or plant

Plant a tree
recreate a history
releasing torrents
> of life-giving rain

upon five hundred
> tired years

of the Christ-opher Columbus
> discovery drought.

My Mother's Poem

*For my beloved mother and in celebration
of progressive African Orature, with all
its sustaining wisdom and aesthetic appeal.*

The day after
                    my father
                    was buried
tormenting images
                            of uncaptured time
                            between him and me
piled up
           on my breaking neck
breathing
           heaviness and sorrow
dragging
           my cracking memory
across gaps
           of lost moments
           of escaped contact.

The day after
                    my father
                    was buried
my space
           in life
was saturated
           with mourning
Unspoken
           torturous thoughts
jettisoned pain
           across
           the warring zone
           of antagonistic
           lost contact.

The day after
                my father
                was buried
the distance
                between home
                and exile
suddenly doubled
and through windows
                            of helplessness
I hurled out
                courage
turning it
                into a heap
                of despair.

The day after
                my father
                was buried
I drowned
                the telephone line
                with rivers of tears
I soaked
                my mother's ears
                with my weeping
I choked
                with lumps
                of words
                trapped in my throat
                as I reached out
                            for dialogue
                            and home.

The day after
                my father
                was buried
My heart could
                no longer
                find a home

                    in exile
So it reached out
                    through the telephone line
                    across the Atlantic
                    to try and touch

my mother

Then came
                the healing words
words embalmed
                with motherly love
words weighted
                with orature wisdom
words spoken
                the day after
                my father
                was buried.

Daughter, do not
romanticize home
Do not, daughter
For many who are home
                        have jail
                        for home
Thousands who are home
                        have streets
                        for home
Millions who are home
                        are crying
                        for home

The whole land
                is crying
                for home
The whole land
                is crying:
                "The waters are bitter
                what shall we drink?"

Daughter, do not
romanticize home
Do not, daughter
You who have

>*chosen the path*
>*of people's struggles*
>*must find the courage*
>*to build new homes*
>*to start new lives*

wherever

>*you are*

be it

>*in the air*

be it

>*on the seas*

be it

>*in the trees*

be it

>*in the desert.*

Create new life
Create human beings

>*out of these*

And build
new homes

On whatever

>*patch of ground*
>*your feet tread*

walk well
step solidly

>*leaving behind you*
>*firm footprints*

walk well
along the path

>*you have chosen*
>*to take.*

The sun shone through
                    the telephone line
its warmth
and brightness
                    lifted the mist
                    that bogged down
                    my vision.

The sun shone through
                    the telephone line

wiping my tears
warming my heart.

The sun shone through
                    the telephone line
releasing
          a flood
          of unchecked
          powerfulness
that lifted me
above the cliff
                    on which I stood
                    overlooking a sea
                    of drowning despair.

The sun shone through
                    the telephone line
                    as I looked beyond
the day after
my father
was buried.

Prosaic Poem

In commemoration of those moments
when we make prosaic statements that
end up sounding poetic and then we are
reminded that ordinary human dialogue
is often punctuated with poetry.

Refrain: One day!

One day,   we shall rescue our lives from precarious peripheral hanging on and assume the center of historical action. We shall explore every avenue that runs through our lives and create live-roads that know no dead ends, extending them to the limits of human destination. We shall put an angry fullstop to the negation of our human rights.

One day!

One day,   we shall undertake a second journey along the bushy path of denied human development, chasing away the wild beasts that prowl the route of our narrow survival lest they make a complete jungle of our already beastialized lives. We shall then cultivate a huge global garden and plant it with the seed of true humanity.

One day!

One day,   We shall emerge from the wings and occupy the center stage in full visibility, refusing to be observers and understudies who wait behind the curtain of living drama. We shall liberate the word and become its utterers, no longer cheer crowds or ululators who spur on and applaud the molestors of our affirmative speech.

One day!

One day,   we shall explode the negative silences and
             paralyzing terror imposed upon us by the tyr-
             anny of dominating cultures and their languages
             of conquest. We shall discover the authentic
             voices of our self-naming and re-naming, reclaim-
             ing our role as composers, speaking for ourselves,
             because we too have tongues, you know!

One day!

One day,   we shall make a bonfire of currently dismantling
             and maladjusting economic structural adjustment
             programmes, then engage in the restructuring
             process, producing coherence around our scat-
             tered daily existence till it is full of bursting. We
             shall stop at nothing short of holding the sun to a
             standstill until the job is complete.

One day!

One day,   we shall move the sun of our existence so that it
             truly rises from the east of our lives, reaching its
             noon at the center of our needs. We shall then
             release it to set in the west of our perverted and
             dominated history, never to rise again until it
             learns to shine upon the masses of global being,
             not on islands of pirated living.

One day!

One day,   we shall exterminate the short distance between
             the kitchen and bedroom of our lives, storm out
             of the suffocating space between the factory and
             the overseer of our exploited creative labour,
             paving a path that leads to the buried mines of
             our suppressed human potential. We shall walk it
             if it stretches unto eternity.

One day!

One day,   we shall celebrate this earth as our home, stand-
             ing tall and short, boasting of the abundance and

84

multifariousness of our fulfilled human visions. We shall not look to the sky waiting for unfulfilled prophecies. We shall upturn the very rocks of our enforced stony existence, converting them into fluvial banks of life sustenance.

One day!